Wha

Right

MARK FINLEY
AND
STEVEN MOSLEY

Pacific Press® Publishing Association
Nampa, Idaho
Oshawa, Ontario, Canada

Edited by B. Russell Holt
Designed by Tim Larson
Cover photo by © digital/STOCK

ISBN 0-8163-1842-5

01 02 03 04 05 • 5 4 3 2 1

Contents

Spelling Out Love

As a parent, you try to show your child so many different things. You try to teach your child so many different things. But what is it that they'll remember the most? What will really stick with them? What will shape them?

Have you ever wondered that? Have you ever wondered what they will look back on most fondly—when they grow up?

You are about to find out. You're about to discover what young people say made the biggest difference in their lives.

There's been a lot written these days in books and magazines about child development. And it's really important. What can a parent do that really sticks with a child, that will really mold a child as he or she grows up? We can do a lot of things as mothers and fathers, of course. But what things count the most? That's a big question. It's perhaps the biggest question for a parent.

In this chapter, we're going to find answers. We're going to find answers from the experts, from healthy kids who are old enough to look back and talk about: "What My Parents Did Right." We decided to interview young people at a Christian college in northern California. Young adults are old enough to look back on their childhood with a little perspective. They've passed through adolescence for the most part; they've been over the bumps of teenage rebellion. But they're also young enough to still feel those bumps. The style of parenting they received is quite fresh in their minds. And right now they're sorting out what's important for their lives, and what's not.

So we asked these kids what made the difference for them. We asked what values have stuck with them. We asked: How did your parents teach you right from wrong? How did your parents try to give you a positive attitude about God and faith?

We'll be looking at answers to those questions in the following chapters in this book. In this chapter, we'll start with another question—one that goes right to the heart of parenting, to the heart of growing up healthy. We asked, "How did your parents make you feel loved?"

Good parents try to communicate love and nurture in a variety of ways. But we wanted to zero in on what had the strongest impact, what made children feel most secure.

Robin Fowler: "I remember my dad would always sing me to sleep every night, from the time I was two until the time I was in eighth grade. It's just a memory I look back on. There are certain songs that trigger my memory and that make me feel good that he took that certain time out of his day to spend with me, to share a piece of his love for music and instill that in me."

Ted Smith: "My mom would take some time during the day and just talk to me, usually right before I went to bed. We'd talk about anything, stuff that had gone on during the day or whatever I wanted to talk about."

Heather Pope: "My dad used to read to me to put me to sleep. I remember he would always fall asleep while he was reading, and really weird things would come out of his mouth! But just the fact that he'd read to me every night, even if I had no idea what he was talking about, was really neat."

These are kids who are looking back over their whole childhood, and what do they remember most fondly? When did they feel most loved? When my dad sang to me. When my mom talked to me. When my dad read to me.

These were the responses that struck us over and over. And you know, all of their responses revolve around one thing in particular. The feeling of being loved, of being secure, is tied in their minds with one certain gift—the gift of time. Counselors and psychologists emphasize the same thing.

Sue Murray: "One of the first things that comes to my mind is a song that says children spell love—T-I-M-E. We live in a society that talks about time-crunching and layering tasks, and so people think they don't have enough time. But I really do believe that the way we show anyone that we love her is by giving her time, time when we have some energy to really be present with her."

Jim Tucker is a psychology professor who has done a great deal of research on how values are transmitted to teenagers. He talks—from personal experience—about what really matters.

Jim Tucker: "Spending time with kids is important. I can remember when I was a teenager and my dad, who worked hard all day at physical labor, would go out with me after supper at night and bat balls to me. I was trying to learn to be a baseball player, and he would bat grounders and flies and spend time, even though he was tired, because he was interested in what I was doing. I can still remember after all these years what caring that showed."

If you want to spell out love for a child, it's spelled T-I-M-E. Nothing communicates love like time. That's what sticks in a child's mind; that's what fills a child's heart.

Vladimir Cretko: "One of the main things my parents used to do, that I appreciate now, is that every night before I went to sleep they would read to me, and they would spend time with me. They would go out of their way, no matter how hard both of them were working, to spend time with me as a child."

Time makes a difference. That's the message these kids are giving us. And it's a point that psychologists have proven valid. Family counselor, Sue Murray, talks about one research psychologist, Stanley Greenspan, who actually set up a laboratory where he could observe parent-child interaction and children's behavior. She talks about what he discovered.

Sue Murray: "One of the things he consistently found is that most childhood behaviors that are problematic to families, especially in young children, have dissipated or disappeared when the parents learned to give their children the kind of time they needed. One of his terms is 'floor time.' He suggests that parents of young children should find twenty minutes to half an hour a day to just be on the floor and let the child set the scene for what the child wants to do."

This you can depend on. When your children are asked, "What did your parents do right?" their answers will center around time, the investment of time.

You know, this is one principle that Jesus Himself taught very forcefully during His life on this earth. It's true that Christ didn't literally father any children. But I believe He can give us some important lessons about effective parenting.

Consider for a moment Christ's mission on this planet. Surely His was the most important assignment ever given to any individual. He had to make salvation possible for every human being. He had to spread the message of His kingdom to the entire world. He had to radically change the course of history. And Jesus had only three short years in which to accomplish this mission.

It's too bad He didn't have satellite TV. It's too bad He couldn't get on the Internet and establish Himself a big Web site. Everybody could have heard quickly, right? That's what many of us would think today. After all, He had to communicate a life-saving message. He had to communicate it in a way that would stick with people after He was gone.

How did He do this? Robert Coleman showed us how some years ago in a book called *The Master Plan of Evangelism.* Coleman pointed out that Jesus Christ's essential strategy was this: He poured His life into twelve human beings. He lived with them; He ate with them; He taught them; He discipled them; He listened to them.

Now, think about it. Christ only had three years in which to do His work. What was His main plan of action? To disciple twelve men. He poured Himself into them until they were able to communicate His message to the world.

Christ invested His time in a few other human beings. That's what our calling is as parents. It's the greatest gift we can give. And it will produce the greatest results—in healthy, secure children.

Now, there are other things that stood out in the things these students said, things that stood out about the *kind* of time spent with them.

Many of their warmest memories had to do with bedtime,

how they were cared for at bedtime. That seems to be especially important for children. It seems to be an especially important moment in their lives. The things that happen to them as they go to sleep seem to make a deep impression on their minds. So investing ourselves, investing our time, as our children go to bed, is especially valuable.

Another thing that stood out, that these students talked about regularly, was the consistent regular time their parents gave them. They talked about the fact that their parents, not only spent time with them, but they did it on a systematic, consistent basis. They didn't look back on one special moment, one great time they had with their parents. They looked back on regular events in their childhood, they looked back on events that became family rituals.

Clifford Lim: "Every night after we had family worship, my parents would always give me a kiss, both of them would always do that. That was something I expected and something they always gave me."

Stacy Neira: "I remember my dad would take a day off work at least once a month and he'd take me on a 'date.' He would take me out to breakfast in the morning, and we'd go shopping, and he'd buy me an outfit or something. It just made me feel really special because he took a day off work to spend with me."

A family ritual helps children feel secure and loved. It's something they can count on. It's something that sets comforting boundaries around their world. When children have that investment of time, then something happens to them when they get older. Something happens to them, when they find out more about the world, when they realize it isn't always so safe, when they experience more conflicts. Secure children are able to come to their parents with all their questions. They can come and get help, get reassurance. They won't be afraid that their parents can't handle it or will react angrily.

Mark Taber: "It was just the general feeling that I really, truly could always go to them with basically anything."

Kendall Ermshar: "They were always there and they were always willing to do whatever it took."

Shawn Kohltfarber: "They were willing to listen to some of the craziest things that I had to offer."

When we invest regular time with our children, we give them a sense that we will always be there. That's an invaluable thing for a child to have. It pays rich dividends. It does something to kids as they grow up. It gives them a certain attitude about their future.

Becky Kendall: "I remember Sabbath mornings and having breakfast in bed with my parents. We would talk about what we wanted to do in the future and family trips that we had taken. That feeling of belonging to a family that loved me so much really gave me a sense of security."

Stacie Fenderson: "Not too long ago, maybe my high school years, my dad and I used to sit up late at night talking about my future. We'd stay up until one or two in the morning, Friday nights, just talking about me."

Ishmael Darjean: "When we were kids, every day when the day was almost done, my mom would always read to us and then tuck us each in at night and just tell us to be great kids. That always felt good, when my mom was tucking me in, because it made me feel special—like I was going somewhere, and I was important to her and in her life."

Notice what this young man said. That nighttime ritual gave him a sense that, "I was going somewhere; I was important." That mother's act of tucking her son in bed said so much. It communicated something to this little boy. He was going to have a positive future. This person cared for him. This person wanted him to be a great kid.

Parents who have the greatest impact are parents who invest time because they *believe* in their kids. They don't just invest time because it's their duty; they don't just invest time because they're supposed to. They invest time because they believe this is an important investment. They believe that this precious life in their hands can blossom into something beautiful.

Charonda Willis: "When I was about five or six, my mother was in the kitchen making tacos. I asked her if I could help, and she said yes. I dropped a taco into the skillet, and hot oil popped into my eye. She grabbed me in her arms and ran to the kitchen sink. She was putting water in my eye. We got in the car, and she raced me to the hospital. The doctor said I would not be able to see out of my left eye. I remember that I didn't cry, but my mother was having a hard time with it. She kept praying with me. Every morning, we'd get up and pray. She took the patch off in about two weeks—and I could see! I'll never forget that. She just stuck with me all the way."

Charonda knew, beyond a shadow of a doubt, that her mother was going to stick with her all the way. Do you know that Jesus gave His disciples that kind of assurance? It came at the end of His three-year investment of pouring His life into the lives of those twelve disciples who would carry on His work.

Matthew records a "Great Commission" that Christ gave His disciples just before ascending to heaven to be reunited with His Father. And it adds some interesting words about His contact with us, not only here on this earth, but always, through eternity. He said, " 'Go therefore and make disciples of all the nations, baptizing them in the name of the Father and of the Son and of the Holy Spirit, teaching them to observe all things that I have commanded you; and lo, I am with you always, even to the end of the age.' " (Matthew 28:19, 20, NKJV).

Christ had entrusted His kingdom, His legacy, into the hands of these twelve men. And He told them that He would always be with them—to the end of time. He would always be there for them.

Shortly after this, Jesus did something that shows how He expressed faith in His disciples, how He believed in them in spite of their shortcomings. Acts, chapter one, describes the scene. Jesus has one last thing to say before He's taken up into the clouds to heaven. He reminds the twelve to wait for the promise of the Holy Spirit. That's how He would continue an intimate relationship with His disciples—through His Spirit living inside of them.

One of the disciples turned to Jesus and asked, "Lord, will you at this time restore the kingdom to Israel?"

Now this question should have been quite a blow to Christ. He had spent three years showing these men exactly what His kingdom was all about. He'd taken pains to show them it was a kingdom of heaven, a kingdom of the heart. It wasn't a matter of restoring a nation; it wasn't about politics. But the disciples still didn't quite get the picture. They couldn't quite let go of their old ideas about the restoration of Israel.

So how did Christ respond at this critical moment? An ordinary man might have thrown up his hands in dismay. How could these people be so dense? An ordinary man would have come down on his disciples for not paying better attention. But Jesus did something else. He expressed faith, an extraordinary faith. He didn't look at their temporary confusion. He looked at their future, their future filled with the Holy Spirit.

And this is what He said: "But you shall receive power when the Holy Spirit has come upon you; and you shall be witnesses to Me in Jerusalem, and in all Judea and Samaria, and to the end of the earth" (Acts 1:8, NKJV).

You will be My witnesses. What a beautiful expression of faith! You will be My witnesses to the end of the earth. Christ believed in His disciples; He believed in these flawed, sinful human beings. He had invested His life in them, and He spoke confidently about their future.

That's the legacy that Christ has given to each one of us. And He has given it to parents in a special way. His faith can be our faith. His confidence can be our confidence.

There are so many ways we can show our children that we believe in them. There is a great legacy we can leave our children. It's built up from little bedtime rituals and from things we do at dinner time and from songs and books and conversations.

But what it requires most of all is an investment of our time. We have to be there; we have to be present; we have to listen; we have to share. Because children spell love T-I-M-E, time.

I'd like you to make a commitment with me right now as a parent. Determine that you're going to make an investment of yourself in the lives of your children. Maybe you're very busy. Maybe your job is terribly demanding right now. Maybe you have to travel a lot, like I do. Perhaps you're going through a divorce, and you're having a more difficult time seeing your kids.

Whatever the obstacle, whatever the challenge, will you decide to make that essential investment of regular time? Will you decide to make it happen, whatever it takes? Ask God to help you put priority on things that will matter, not only today, but for eternity. Why not ask God to help you put your priority on your children?

A Winning Example

Every parent wants to teach his child right from wrong. Every parent wants to communicate values. But how do we do that in a way that sticks with them? What can we say that they'll still remember when they are eighteen or twenty?

In this chapter, we'll find out. You're going to learn just what eighteen- and twenty-year-olds really do remember most.

Robin Matsukawa: "One of the main things I remember about my mother as I was growing up was that she always gave gifts, no matter what the financial situation. Being a single mother, she didn't have easy access to much money, but she always gave gifts."

Brandon Franklin: "One thing, especially, that my dad has always stressed, is honesty. He's always set a good example with that too. He's honest in everything he does."

Tarun Kapoor: "I grew up in India, and there were a lot of poor people who would come by, but my parents would ask me to invite them into the house and offer them food and help them. They would go to the local communities and help people and just treat everybody the same, whether they were my relatives or not. I'd give them the same respect. That has made me a really compassionate person, and I thank them for that."

We talked to quite a few college-age students, asking them what made the greatest impact in their learning right from wrong. And what they pointed out, over and over again, was not just something their parents *said;* it was something their parents *did.* They remembered a quality that their mom or dad exhibited in daily life. That's what stuck with them—what their parents practiced.

These kids zeroed in on one basic thing—a winning example.

Robin Fowler: "I just remembered them being examples for me, and their example just instilled in my mind what was right and wrong."

Kendall Ermshar: "What my parents did mostly was to teach through example."

Actions are what kids will use as building blocks. That's what they'll use when they start sorting out their own values, when they start shaping their own sense of right and wrong. It's not what you preach over and over that counts in the end; it's what you practice over and over. Counselors and psychologists who have studied how values are transmitted reinforce this essential point.

Roger Dudley: "Information alone isn't all that helpful in developing values; neither is punishment effective, or coercion. Among the things that are most effective is—for one thing—the example of the parents. Kids are very influenced by what they see in their parents' lives. If parents have a code of integrity and high moral standards and live by those standards, even though the kids may seem to be rejecting and rebelling against them, yet they are influenced by that; it has an ongoing influence in their lives."

Jim Tucker: "It seems to me that parents communicate values best by their own behavior, by their own words, by their own example. We parents behave in certain ways, and our children see through us if we are hypocritical in any way. They will be more likely to do what we do than they will be to do what we say they should do."

Counselors are all saying it. It's difficult to instill a set of values in your child if your lifestyle doesn't back it up.

Kids, looking back, are all saying it too. A parent's example makes the greatest difference. That's what makes an impact. That's what sticks with them. You know, the greatest moral Teacher in history taught in this way. He taught in the way of example. Jesus taught His disciples by His own example, by His own actions. These actions reinforced Christ's words.

He called His disciples to become fishers of men, because He was the world's greatest Fisher of men.

He could ask them to forsake everything else because He had forsaken everything to come to this earth as a human being.

He could ask them to take up their cross because He would take up the cross for all of us.

He could ask them to love their neighbor as themselves because He poured out His love day after day.

Jesus gives us that example. He tells us that we can be examples, too, when we minister in His name. We are following in His footsteps. That's the privilege of every believer, and it's the privilege of every parent. None of us are perfect. The twelve disciples certainly weren't. They were chosen, but they weren't perfect. They were weak human beings who often had a hard time understanding what Christ's kingdom was all about. They sometimes got caught up in rivalries and petty quarrels. But they were trying to follow this extraordinary Teacher, Jesus Christ. And as a result, they changed the course of history.

Powerful things happen when we, too, lead by example.

One of the great benefits of leading by example, of teaching by example, is this: As they get older, kids are better able to make good decisions for themselves. They've seen a winning example. It's not just something they've been ordered to do or told that they have to do; it's something they've seen demonstrated, day after day, week after week, month after month in practical life. They're able to choose values that they have seen working in their parents' lives.

And choice is important when it comes to a solid sense of right and wrong. In fact, we don't really develop a moral compass without it.

Becky Kendall: "I think instead of *telling* me what was right and what was wrong, my parents *showed* me. They were excellent examples through their lives. And it was never like they said, 'Becky, don't do this or don't do that.' Of course they did that in some instances, but as I grew older and started making decisions for myself, I based my decisions on the life that I'd seen my parents live."

Jessica Shine: "I think one of the ways they taught me about their love is that they gave me freedom of choice, and they allowed me to choose for myself and to learn from my mistakes."

Ishmael Darjean: "My mom would always use the Bible as her yardstick, and she'd always tell us, 'You know what's right.' Then she'd leave us to make decisions for ourselves."

This is the other thing these college kids emphasized when we asked them about what their parents did right in teaching them right from wrong. They kept referring to choice, to the opportunity to begin making decisions on their own.

After all, that's the only way values can be internalized. Sometimes parents forget that. We get stuck in the parenting style that worked when our kids were little, when we had to keep them from running out into the traffic and tell them what they could touch and what they couldn't.

Sometimes we don't want to let go of that absolute authority, that control. Letting our kids have more and more independence is a very scary thing. We're afraid of what might happen. We're afraid of the wrong choices that they might make.

But values don't become our own until we freely choose them. Each of us has to decide what principles we're going to live by.

Barry Gane: "Some of the studies that we've done, fairly extensive studies, have shown that the more independence cradled by love that's given to teenagers, the more likely they are to adopt the value system of their parents."

Roger Dudley: "Parents need to show their kids how to take value-making into decisions. So that instead of simply a list of what's right and wrong, you take a real situation, something we sometimes call a moral dilemma, and you look at that and say, 'What should I do in that situation or what should the participants do?' Then you decide what principles could apply and how you can work through to a decision."

Remember that, at a certain point, Jesus Christ, sent His disciples out on their own. He'd poured His life into them; He'd taught them the principles of His kingdom. And now He challenged them to try out those principles in the real world. They had to see for themselves that "turn the other cheek" really worked. They had to see for themselves that they could receive God's power in healing the sick.

Our children need the same freedom, too. They need it especially as they get older. They have to have space in which to test our values in the real world. And yes, they have to learn from their mistakes.

But there are things we can do, as parents, to ease that transition into the outside world. We can lay a foundation for that time. We can give our children some good equipment, some tools with which to sort out values. We can do that by *explaining* our values, *explaining* why we believe the way we do, instead of just telling our kids what to do.

Professor and family counselor Sue Murray teaches behavioral sciences at Andrews University. She talks about why in these days we have a special need for explaining our values to our children.

Sue Murray: "One of the things we've found out is that children will often say that they know their grandparents' values—what's important to their grandparents—more than they know what's important to their parents. I've been a part of some discussions as to why that is and have done some reading. One of the reasons may be because many baby boomer parents aren't particularly comfortable with their past and what they did in their youth. They don't want their kids to behave that way or to make those choices. So they haven't shared very much about their own experience. And so kids don't really know what their parents value."

Your kids need to know where you stand. They need to know why you believe certain choices are best. Your past doesn't have to be perfect in order for you to talk about what's best for them. You have learned from your mistakes. Your kids can learn from your mistakes as well. They don't have to know all the details. But it would help them to know what has worked in your life, and what hasn't. Kids want to know why. They need an honest explanation.

Barry Gane: "It's really not effective for a parent to say 'You've got to do this because I'm telling you to do it.' That works for a little while, but the older the child gets the more he wants the parent to explain *why* this is a value—what is important about it, how does it fit into the overall scheme of things? That's probably as important as anything else."

Emily Moran: "I didn't know that our family didn't have a lot of rules. My parents talked about natural consequences more than right and wrong, and how God has provided all these open doors for opportunity. Choosing our own way is actually kind of *not* an opportunity; it's kind of like sticking in one spot and not going anywhere. My parents have always been very positive about that stuff—not so much emphasizing the negative as the positive. And that's really great. I love my parents so much."

What a wonderful legacy to leave with your kids! This young lady has a positive picture of the good life. She sees God's way as a way of opportunity, a way of going somewhere.

Natalie Yialelis: "My mom does random acts of kindness. Sends extra food for my friends, etc."

Barry Gane: "Consistency in the parent's life is essential. It's very difficult for a parent to instill a set of values in a child that is different from the lifestyle that they themselves are living. All of us are hypocrites to some extent, so we're not consistent all the time. But a level of consistency is necessary if we're going to propose a set of values and expect a young person to adopt them."

Communicating positive values makes a bigger impact than just communicating about what's wrong. Talking about opportunities makes a bigger impact than warning about dangers. Yes, we do have to tell our kids about destructive habits and negative influences. But that isn't what should dominate our perspective. We should talk about something else—much, much more. Talk about the good things there are in life. Talk about the opportunities God opens up for each of His children. Talk about the benefits of following God's plan. Explaining why we have certain values helps a lot. Positive explanations help the most.

You know, Jesus Christ took great pains to paint a positive picture of the kingdom of heaven for His disciples. He wanted them to see the great potential of that kingdom. He wanted them to see limitless possibilities. Read this classic picture in Matthew. It's here that Jesus describes the kingdom in glowing terms: " 'The kingdom of heaven is like a mustard seed, which a man took and sowed in his field, which indeed is the least of all the seeds; but when it is grown it is greater than the herbs and becomes a tree, so that the birds of the air come and nest in its branches' " (Matthew 13:31, 32, NKJV).

A tiny seed that grows into a wonderful, shady tree— that's the picture Jesus wanted His disciples to see. The kingdom of heaven is something that expands our lives. It doesn't make them smaller. It's something that stretches us, something that makes us fruitful.

Jesus gave His disciples other bright pictures as well. The kingdom of heaven is like a pearl of great price that is worth selling everything else for. The kingdom of heaven is like a treasure hidden in a field. The kingdom of heaven can make us the salt of the earth; it can make us a bright light set on a hill.

Jesus explained the values of the kingdom in a way

that made people want to invest themselves in it. They wanted to pursue it. And that kingdom has stood the test of time. That kingdom continues to give shelter, like a great spreading tree. It continues to light up the world. It continues to produce people who are the salt of the earth.

That's what we can do in sharing our own personal values with our children. We can do it, first of all, by example. We can let our actions speak loudest. And we can do it by explaining why we've adopted certain values; we can talk about why they work for us. We can tell our children why they work for us. We give our kids a positive picture of what their life can be like as they follow God's principles.

And the most important principle we share—the most important value we can communicate—is unconditional love. That's so important to share when we are trying to teach our children right from wrong. Because it's not easy to let our kids start making their own decisions. It's not easy giving up that complete control. We over-react when our kids disappoint us. We make them feel rejected at times. We want to *make* them follow that straight and narrow path.

But in doing that we deny them the most important value of all—the value of love. After all, God sacrificed everything in order to give us freedom of choice. He gave up His one and only Son in order to enable us to choose salvation.

We do need to give our children boundaries as they grow up. We do need to set definite limits when our kids are little. But the most important boundary for them to have is the knowledge that they will never, never wander beyond the reach of our love—the knowledge that our love will always be there to draw them back home.

Sue Murray: "I just heard someone recently say that he grew up in a family that was quite health conscious.

He knew that smoking was not an option for him. He lived in a community where he had the message that smoking was not an OK thing to do. And yet he found himself, with some of his friends, developing a habit of smoking. He was a teenager when that came to his mother's attention. She reached across to him and planted a kiss on his forehead, and she said, 'No matter what you ever do, I will always love you.' And he said, 'I never smoked again.' He said, 'It was my mother's grace that made the difference for me.' "

What legacy are you going to leave your children? What values will stick with them as they grow up and leave the nest?

By God's grace we can leave them an example, an honest attempt to live out our convictions. By God's grace we can give them something to hang onto. We can give them a positive picture of the good life, a positive picture of God's principles and the joy and the happiness they bring.

Will you dedicate yourself to that great task? Will you dedicate yourself to showing your children which way is best? Will you dedicate yourself right now, to say, "Jesus, I may have failed as a parent at times, I may not have been the example that I should have been. I may look back on times with some regrets. But Lord, I want to make a new commitment to always be painting that positive picture of You for my children. I want to make a new commitment of loving my children no matter what."

Do you want to say, "God, I want to be a positive example of Your way of life, radiating the happiness and joy that You can only bring"?

Making It Personal

Of all the gifts we can give our children, none is more important, none has more wide-ranging effects, than the gift of knowing God. And yet spirituality is one of the hardest things to pass along to the next generation. It's hard to pin down; it's easy to let it slip away.

In this chapter, we'll hear from kids who got the greatest gift from their parents—and who hung onto it.

We don't just naturally inherit a relationship with God. Spirituality isn't something easily handed down from one person to another, from one generation to another, like a photo album. And yet, there is no more important legacy we can give our children. We want them to have a spiritual life. We want them to have a healthy relationship with God. How do we share that with our children? Parents struggle a lot with that question. What's the best way to give our kids a positive attitude about God and faith?

We decided to find answers by talking to kids who've grown up a bit. We found students at a Christian college who do feel positive about the faith their parents passed on to them, students who feel good about their relationship with God. And we asked them, "What did your parents do right when it came to passing on the faith?"

Chris Chang: "My mom's a pretty devoted Christian. She reads her Bible every morning. Just seeing what she does—going to church and praying—I learn a lot by seeing her actions."

Christian Mason: "We kind of had a ritual. Until I was about ten, every night my dad would tell us a Bible story, and he'd pray with us. So I knew all the Bible stories and a bunch of texts. Yeah, they were good about that."

Natalie Yialelis: "My mom would send me lunch. She used to pack my lunch, even up through high school. And she'd send extra food for my friends. She'd make cookies and just did random acts of kindness that showed me God's love. Because we don't deserve it. It's definitely a grace."

Jeffery Johnson: "I can remember when I was growing up, I'd get up in the morning and I would walk past my dad, and he'd be leaning over the couch, reading the Bible or praying. And I'd see my mom at the kitchen table eating her breakfast, reading the Bible. I could see in their lives that spending that time with God in the morning was really important to them. We'd always have family worship together. I think that's how they encouraged me. I could see it working in their lives. God was important in their lives, and that's one of the reasons I wanted God to be important in my life."

"I could see it working in their lives." That's the response that hit us over and over again. Kids absorbed what they saw working. And what sunk in most deeply was the personal faith that they saw their parents practice. They saw their parents invest energy in an individual relationship with God.

Dr. Roger Dudley was involved in a study of 1,500 teenagers to determine why they accepted or rejected the religion of their parents.

Roger Dudley: "Kids are very influenced when they see the devotion that their parents have and by the fact that they know their parents pray, that they know their parents attend church regularly and spend time reading the Bible."

Habits of personal devotion make a big impact—not only on our lives, but on the lives of our children. There's really no substitute for that. You can't go to church enough or do enough religious things to make up for a lack of a personal devotional life.

Another thing we discovered is that kids respond positively when parents show them that this personal faith can have a practical impact in their lives.

Becky Kendall: "In the tough decisions that I faced in life, my parents really led me to look toward God and to pray and to trust that He would ultimately show me the way."

Showing our kids that God is a very present help in time of need makes a difference. We need to bring God down to ground level. He can't just remain an abstraction in the sky, a distant figure we acknowledge out of duty. We need to show our kids that God can be very close. Sometimes we show that best when times get real tough.

Charonda Willis: "My mother has been on disability for four years now, and she has never had any negative attitude about it. She has always kept the faith in God. Whenever she or my father face trials and tribulations, they don't get upset with God. They just go and pray. And they always keep the faith. My mother is always saying, 'God will make a way somehow.' And He always does. So seeing how they deal with problems and troubles encourages me to have faith in God."

Jesus Christ actually did some wonderful parenting while He was on this earth. He gave us some great lessons in how to parent effectively by the way He discipled the twelve men He poured His life into. And one of the things He did was to show them how dependent He Himself was on His heavenly Father. He wanted the disciples to understand that His strength, His power, flowed directly from God. Listen to what He told them, " 'I tell you the truth, the Son can do nothing by himself; he can do only what he sees his Father doing, because whatever the Father does the Son also does. For the Father loves the Son and shows him all he does' " (John 5:19, 20, NIV).

Jesus Christ, the great Messiah, the great Miracle-Worker, wanted His disciples to know who He relied on, who He prayed to, day by day. He consistently gave credit to His heavenly Father. In fact, He was always trying to get the disciples to see the Father through Him. He says, " 'The words that I speak to you I do not speak on My own authority; but the Father who dwells in Me does the works' " (John 14:10, NKJV). Jesus kept pointing to the Father who dwelled in Him, the Father who could dwell in each one of His followers through the Spirit. Jesus consistently identified His very life with the life of His heavenly Father.

In picturing Himself as the Good Shepherd, Jesus said this about the Father: " 'My sheep hear My voice, and I know them, and they follow Me. And I give them eternal life, and they shall never perish; neither shall anyone snatch them out of My hand. My Father, who has given them to Me, is greater than all; and no one is able to snatch them out of My Father's hand' " (John 10:27-29, NKJV).

Jesus Christ gave His disciples a great sense of security. He assured them that nothing could snatch them out of the Father's hands. He always pointed to the One they could rely on. That's what each of us can do as a parent, too. That's the lesson that will have a long-term impact in the lives of our own children. One young woman told us about something her dad shared with her. He wanted her to always remember three things about God: (1) He's all-knowing; (2) He's loving; and (3) His character is one of infinite goodness and grace. That knowledge became a source of strength one day when she was feeling exhausted, and facing a very difficult examination.

Carol Britton: "In the middle of my exam, I came to a test question and I just thought, 'This is going to do me in.' I went to God, and I repeated all three things my dad had taught me about God. I said, 'God, I'm going to call on Your promise. I need an A on this exam to get past this class.' And I got an A-minus! And it's all because of my dad. He was constantly there telling me, 'Trust God; depend on God.'"

Trust God. Depend on God. That's the same message Christ's disciples absorbed to such good effect. Jesus showed them that the heavenly Father would indeed come through, that He could be trusted to care for our needs. In His Sermon on the Mount, Jesus put it this way: "'Look at the birds of the air, for they neither sow nor reap nor gather into barns; yet your heavenly Father feeds them. Are you not of more value than they?'" (Matthew 6:26, NKJV).

You are valuable in God's eyes. That's a lesson Christ kept reinforcing through His words and through His life. He also asked His followers to look out at the meadows, to look at the lilies of the field and consider how beautifully they are clothed. "If God adorns the flowers with such bright colors," He said, "surely He can be relied on to provide you with clothing and shelter."

Christ the Parent wanted His children, His disciples, to understand clearly that they could come to the heavenly Father with any need at any time. He promised that if they just asked, if they just knocked, the Father would answer. " 'If a son asks for bread from any father among you, will he give him a stone? Or if he asks for a fish, will he give him a serpent instead of a fish? Or if he asks for an egg, will he offer him a scorpion? If you then, being evil, know how to give good gifts to your children, how much more will your heavenly Father give the Holy Spirit to those who ask Him!' " (Luke 11:11-13, NKJV).

God knows how to give us good gifts. God knows how to care for us. That's the lesson which sunk deep into the disciples' hearts and minds. And that's the lesson that will sink deep into our children. It's something they can carry with them into adulthood.

Above all, kids need to see a religion that works, a faith that functions. And many times we don't make that picture clear enough—because we don't really let our kids in on what's happening inside of us. We don't let them see how God is really working.

Roger Dudley: "Parents need to share their personal faith with their kids. A large study showed that many parents are hesitant to talk about personal faith with their kids. They can tell their kids what to do and can talk abstractly, but to talk about what God means in their own life and what God has done for them and what Jesus means to them personally is something a lot of parents don't do. And yet it's that personal sharing that has an effect in transmitting faith."

Sue Murray: "It seems to me that often it is easier for us to talk about our spiritual journeys and our spiritual values to people outside of the family than to those inside the family. And I wonder if that is partly because it's a very vulnerable thing to do. But I think children need to know when you believe a prayer has been answered, when you saw God working in your life as a youth, the way that God's teachings have helped you make decisions for yourself, some of the mistakes that you have made, some of the regrets you have. They don't need the details necessarily, but I think they really need to know that their parents are real people who have a living, growing faith with God."

Sharing honestly about our own spiritual journey enables our children to begin their own spiritual journey. And it's an individual journey of discovery for each of us. One of the things that the students we talked to kept bringing up was the fact that they had to make the journey on their own. It's not something that you can really embark on just because your parents want you to. Listen to what the parents of these kids did right:

Heather Pope: "When I was young, my parents always took me to church, but church was never something that was forced on me. Starting in junior high and into high school, it was all my decision to go to church."

Kendall Ermshar: "My parents didn't force religion upon us, which I think allowed me to have a positive image of God because whenever anything is forced, your natural reaction is to rebel."

Faith can't be forced, of course. It has to be a natural response to the love and grace of God. Sometimes, in our zeal to pass on the faith, that basic fact passes us by.

Sue Murray: "It seems to me that lots of conservative Christian parents are so determined that their children will be Christians that in spite of all their well-meaning, they drive their kids away. And then they're so sad, and their kids are left with guilt. The bottom line is that each of us has to accept a personal relationship with Christ. We can't make our child do that. But we can provide an environment that will help them want to find that way."

Every individual is a unique creation of God. Every individual has his or her own temperament and personality. The same things that inspired your spiritual growth may not inspire your child's. The same things that made you feel close to God may not work for your children. Everyone has to find his own particular, deep relationship with God. The basic faith we're affirming is, of course, the same. The God of heaven we worship is the same. But we can lift our hearts up to Him in different ways.

What does come through consistently, however, in what these college kids report, is that we have to make the life of faith an enjoyable experience. It can't just be a duty; it can't just be a chore. With a little effort you can create great spiritual memories for your children, great memories that they'll associate with a positive faith. You can create a happy setting, a good atmosphere in which to share the things that matter most.

Clifford Lim: "My parents encouraged me to participate in church. We did plays as a kid in church. They'd always encourage me to do it and take me to practice sessions here and there. Obviously they encouraged me to read my Bible every morning. Just being involved in church—I think that's helped me a lot. And sending me to schools where I could get a Christian education—that's definitely helped."

Kids remember most what they freely participate in most. They remember the good times. And one of the most powerful things we can do as parents is to connect our personal faith with the good times.

Stacie Fenderson: "My parents were always active in the church, singing up front, etc. And they always made sure I was really involved which made it fun. So that was part of my first impression of God."

Mark Taber: "A lot of people have a hard time with religion because they just see it as a lot of work. My parents never conveyed it as work to me, so I don't feel that it's work."

I think that sums it up very well. Don't make religion seem like work. Make it a natural, joyful part of life; make it a part of the good times that your family enjoys together.

Give your children the opportunity to make suggestions, to express faith in their own way. Give them a chance to stretch their wings in a world created by a loving God. You can create a picture in your kids' minds of the life of faith as a life of great adventure. You can give them that perspective.

That's what Jesus did for His disciples. He called these simple fishermen to follow Him and become fishers of men. He called them to a grand task. He challenged them to set out on a journey of discovery with Him, to be part of a great movement. God is big enough to excite our kids' imaginations. His calling is high enough to touch their deepest ideals. His principles are sound enough to give them a fulfilling life.

That's the picture our kids need to see. That's the vision that they need to catch.

Let's give them that most important legacy. Let's make sure we have a personal faith to pass on. Let's make sure we are practicing the faith we're trying to share. Let's dedicate ourselves, for our children's sake, to Christ, to His kingdom, to show the love of God. For our children's sake, let's make that deep commitment right now.

The Father Behind the Cross

It was World War I, and it was a horrifying introduction to what weapons in the Machine Age could do. Wave after wave of infantry assaults, one artillery barrage after another, one tank attack after another—the fighting went back and forth. And Europe's muddy trenches filled with casualties.

So much carnage. So many men cut down in their prime. So many stories coming to a tragic end. Many people lost their faith after World War I. And yet out of this tragic conflict comes one story, one remarkable story, that can make believers out of us all.

Rudyard Kipling liked to take his children for picnics in the hills of Sussex Downs. He played games with them for hours, and he told them stories. The great British author had fascinated countless readers with tales of life in far-away India, where he had grown up. He would become world-famous with the publication of *The Jungle Book* and *Just So Stories*. But nothing gave him greater satisfaction than telling his own children stories, like the story of how the leopard got his spots and the zebra his stripes. They wanted to hear that story over and over again.

Kipling adored his two daughters, Josephine and Elsie. And when his wife, Carrie, bore him a third child, he was overjoyed when the doctor called out, "You have a son."

Now, the family was complete. Kipling was determined to give his children a happy childhood, one very unlike his own. Rudyard had to be separated from his parents at the tender age of six. He and his sister said farewell to their parents in Bombay and were shipped off to England where they could attend "proper" schools. The woman paid to board them had a mean streak. She would beat and taunt Rudyard, who was small and frail for his age. Sometimes, he was locked in a cold, damp cellar for hours. Years later, Kipling determined that his kids were going to have plenty of sunshine. He enjoyed watching them grow up, playing on the grassy knolls of Sussex.

Kipling took special pride in his son, John. He'd always been a bright, cheerful, uncomplaining child. And he developed into a tall, handsome boy, who loved to play rugby. Kipling loved watching his son dashing across the field. He was a very proud father—not just because John was a great athlete, but because he showed a quiet courage and a good humor. The boy never bragged about a win or whined about a loss.

Kipling realized that his boy was becoming a man and that he was living out the values he'd taught him. Rudyard Kipling always remembered the British servicemen stationed in India. He admired their courage, sacrifice, and discipline. Even in the early 1900s, Kipling was a rather old-fashioned father, emphasizing honor and dedication to duty. And now, he saw John accepting responsibility for his actions. If he broke a rule at school, he took his punishment without complaint, even when it was harsh.

One winter day in 1910, Kipling began to pen some thoughts for his twelve-year-old son. He wanted to express certain ideals to live by. The result was a poem called "IF" which would inspire millions. It ended with these words:

"If you can talk with crowds and keep your virtue,
Or walk with Kings—nor lose the common touch,
If neither foes nor loving friends can hurt you,
If all men count with you, but none too much;
If you can fill the unforgiving minute
With sixty seconds worth of distance run,
Yours is the earth and everything that's in it,
And—what is more—you'll be a man, my son!"

John Kipling did grow up to be a man. And in 1915, with a war raging in Europe, he decided to do his part. His father managed to get him a commission as a second lieutenant with the Irish Guards. But then, came news of heavy casualties in the trenches. Wave after wave of recruits were sailing across the channel to France. John might be called to go over any time now. He was eager to serve, but he was only 17. He required parental consent to go to the front lines.

Rudyard Kipling faced a difficult choice.

He'd visited the front; he'd written about the fighting; he didn't want his son to have to go into that carnage. And yet, everything he'd taught the boy about duty and never shirking responsibility was moving John in that direction.

Rudyard Kipling had been warning about German aggression for years. Now his son wanted to back up his father's words with action. So Kipling gave his consent. On August 15, John waved goodbye from the railing of a ship with a tip of his officer's cap. His mother thought he looked "very smart and straight and brave."

It was the last time his family would ever see him.

Six weeks later a telegram from the War office reported—John Kipling, missing in action. Last seen during a battle in Loos, France. Rudyard Kipling was heartbroken. He tried desperately to learn something, anything, about his son's fate. Traveling over to France, he trudged from one muddy outpost hospital to another. He searched among the wounded. He hunted down men from John's battalion. But he never found his son. He'd been lost in the Great War.

Later, Rudyard Kipling would try to deal with his grief by working with the Imperial War Graves Commission. He proposed that a "Stone of Sacrifice" be erected at each cemetery honoring the war dead. It would represent soldiers whose bodies were never identified. It would be inscribed with these words: "Known But Unto God."

Known But Unto God. That memorial was a father's anguished hope that God did know about that lost son. That God did understand.

I'd like to suggest that God does know, far more than we can ever imagine. Because He too, watched a beloved Son grow into maturity. He too endured a tragedy. He too has a story to tell and a memorial to erect. It's a memorial for each one of us.

When Jesus of Nazareth began to increase in wisdom and stature and in favor with everyone, as Luke tells us, Joseph was proud of his fine Son. But he wasn't the only one. There was another Father, hidden from sight, watching over this Boy. There was a heavenly Father who treasured every step His divine Son took toward becoming a Man.

And one day, this Father just couldn't contain His pride. It burst out at the Jordan River, at the moment when John the Baptist lifted Jesus out of the water of baptism.

Matthew's Gospel describes that event this way: "And suddenly a voice came from heaven, saying, 'This is My beloved Son, in whom I am well pleased.' " (Matthew 3:17, NKJV). God the Father was well pleased with His beloved Son—and He had to tell people about it.

Jesus was beginning His ministry. He was responding to the call of duty. He would teach the multitudes and heal the sick and comfort the afflicted throughout Judea and Galilee. He would live out the principles of grace and love and truth that His Father in heaven had instilled in Him. He would mirror God's character so well that He could say, "If you've seen Me, you've seen the Father."

Yes, this was a Son to be proud of.

But one day, three years later, the heavenly Father had to face a terrible choice. Jesus was agonizing in the Garden of Gethsemane. He was facing a terrible ordeal ahead. He had to make a great sacrifice in the war between good and evil. He had to take on the sins of the world in His own body. It was the only way to make people free.

The Father had watched Him walk steadily toward His rendezvous with destiny in Jerusalem. He would not shirk His responsibility. But now, in that garden, the Son of God crumbled to the ground. The weight of sin seemed overwhelming. Sweating great drops of blood, He cried out, " 'Father, if it is Your will, remove this cup from Me; nevertheless not My will, but Yours, be done' " (Luke 22:42, NKJV).

In those moments, Jesus couldn't see beyond that cup of divine wrath against sin. He only felt a terrible separation from His beloved Father. He wondered if there was some other way out.

And the heavenly Father had to make a terrible choice. He didn't want to see His Son suffer. He didn't want to see Him beaten and mocked and spit upon. He didn't want to see Him tortured at Golgotha. He would have done anything to spare His beloved Son from that agony.

And yet, everything that this Father and Son believed in, everything they stood for, everything they cherished, was moving them toward the Cross. They had made a pact with each other long before; they had resolved to do whatever it took to rescue human beings from sin and death. And it was going to take this. It was going to take the Cross.

That's the terrible choice this Father had to make.

Most of us are familiar with images of Christ's sufferings on the cross, nailed between two thieves. Many have painted vivid pictures of what He must have gone through, totally rejected by man, apparently abandoned by heaven. But, there was another One who suffered too, hidden in the shadows. There was a Father who gave up His Son into our calloused hands. There was a Father who had to watch silently as His Son was brutalized.

He was wounded, too, deeply wounded. His Son was lost, terribly lost. Hell had closed in around Him like some great war that swallows up the noblest and the bravest.

Rudyard Kipling knew a little bit about that kind of sorrow. He knew about it as he wandered from one muddy hospital to another in France, looking for some word of John, his one and only son. He felt that wound when he realized the boy had disappeared without a trace.

The heavenly Father had to watch His Son be consumed by sin, torn apart by transgression. He had to turn away when His Boy cried out, "My God, My God, why have You forsaken Me?"

A father doesn't forget a cry like that. Those words are seared into his memory. Yes, there was a Father behind the Cross, there was One who suffered in the shadows. And do you realize that it's God the Father who turned the cross into a monument? Yes, He had to have a monument for His Son's sacrifice, as did Rudyard Kipling.

"My Son gave up His life for you." That's the inscription on the cross. All the sacrifice that the cross represents is "Known But Unto God." But God wants us to know about that monument. He wants us to know what it means, why it was necessary, and what it can do for us.

During the dark days of World War I, Rudyard Kipling had a hard time coming to terms with his loss. He began to wonder if the death of his son had any meaning at all.

Had it made any difference? The fighting dragged on and on.

One day, Kipling received a rumpled, brown-paper package in the mail. It was addressed simply to Monsieur Kipling. The painstaking scrawl indicated it had been sent from the front.

Kipling opened the package, and there he found a red box inside. It contained a French translation of his novel *Kim*. And the book had been pierced by a bullet hole— that stopped at the last twenty pages. A string had been tied through the hole, and dangling from it was the Maltese Cross, France's medal for bravery in war. It belonged to a young, French soldier named Maurice. He explained in a letter that Kipling's book had saved his life. Had it not been in his pocket when he went into battle, the bullet would have pierced his own heart. Maurice asked Kipling to accept the book and the medal as tokens of his gratitude.

Rudyard Kipling had received many honors as a celebrated British author. He'd even received the Nobel Prize for literature. But no honor moved him as much as this one. God had made him a part of sparing someone's life. Maybe there was a meaning to it all. Maybe there was a point to all the sacrifice.

And that is the point to the sacrifice Jesus made. That is the meaning that the heavenly Father sees. Someone's life can be spared. Your life can be spared. Many lives can be spared.

This is what the writer of Hebrews says as he explains the meaning of Christ's sacrifice on the cross. He presents it as a way to rescue all of God's frail, human children: "Inasmuch then as the children have partaken of flesh and blood, He Himself likewise shared in the same, that through death He might destroy him who had the power of death, that is, the devil, and release those who through fear of death were all their lifetime subject to bondage" (Hebrews 2:14, 15, NKJV).

We're all trapped in a great war on this planet; we're all vulnerable in our flesh and blood. But Christ's sacrificial death destroys the enemy. His perfect life poured out for us, covers our guilt. The enemy, who constantly wars against God, can no longer accuse us. He can no longer hold death over our heads. Christ gives us the right to eternal life.

Listen to Paul talk about this great deliverance: "Grace to you and peace from God the Father and our Lord Jesus Christ, who gave Himself for our sins, that He might deliver us from this present evil age, according to the will of our God and Father, to whom be glory forever and ever. Amen" (Galatians 1:3-5, NKJV).

God the Father and God the Son were together in that sacrifice, in that giving of themselves. That's why we can be delivered from an evil age into the Kingdom of Heaven.

Paul the apostle knew what a privilege it is to be rescued. He knew the part the Father played in the drama of redemption. And so, he wanted to give God the Father glory forever and ever. He wanted God to know the depth of his gratitude. He wanted to turn the monument of the cross into a medal that the Father holds in His hands, a medal that says, "You've saved this life; I'm forever grateful."

Do you see the Father behind the Cross today? Do you understand the depth of His sacrifice? What honor can you give Him today, as a token of your gratitude?

With a Father in the shadows of the Cross, allowing His Son to have nails through His hands and a crown of thorns upon His head and blood running down His face, with a Father demonstrating that kind of love, how can you turn away? How can you turn your back on that love?

Rudyard Kipling and the French soldier, Maurice, kept

up a correspondence over the years. They developed a friendship that helped Kipling deal with the loss of his own son. One day, Maurice wrote that his wife had given birth to a baby boy. Would Kipling consent to be the godfather? Kipling looked out his study window. And he remembered that joyful moment when he first held his own son in his arms. Now Maurice knew that magical feeling—because his life had been spared. And Kipling realized that no memorial would do more justice to his brave son's memory than this tiny infant, full of promise.

So he wrote back, saying he'd be delighted. Rudyard Kipling became the child's godfather. Maurice named him, Jean, French for John. And Kipling presented the infant with a gift, that book with the bullet hole in it and the Maltese Cross, Maurice's medal. He thought it only fitting that the child should have it.

Do you know what gives God the Father His greatest joy? Do you know what He finds most rewarding about the sacrifice He and His Son made? It's seeing many other children born into faith, born again into the kingdom of heaven. That's what makes it all worthwhile.

God enables us to clutch the Cross in our hands as a medal. He wants us to know it was worth it, just to see the light come on in His child's eyes.

Have you received that honor from the Father? Do you know what it costs to give you this privilege? What it means to be welcomed as a child of God?

I invite you to respond to this Father's love right now. I invite you to say, yes, to the most wondrous sacrifice ever made. Will you make that decision in your heart? Will you reach out to the Father and be rescued right now?

Being Married to Me

"I mean you should have known, Alice. I phoned you twice. You don't check the answering machine now?"

Alice: "It's almost ready."

"Dinner could have been ready five minutes ago. Now I have to wait. You know, I've got to start drinking milk—you're going to give me an ulcer. I just don't believe it. The bathroom towels are wrinkled. I found a slipper on the living room floor. You didn't hang up my bathrobe, and you know how I feel about that. You can't even clean the house. You know, you don't work full time; I don't know what you do with all the time you've got. Sometimes I just don't understand how after all these years you still don't know how to do it right. I really just don't understand you sometimes."

Gary Smallnik has been Alice's husband for thirteen years. He's had a lot of time to think. Unfortunately, he's never asked himself one question: What's it like being married to me?

People sink into very bad habits when they don't ask themselves a very important question: "What's it like being married to me?" That question becomes extremely critical after a marriage has gone through many years of wear and tear. Let's look at a typical example.

43

Jack and Lisa had just celebrated their fifteenth wedding anniversary. It was a nice occasion; friends came over to wish them well. They had a nice dinner together. They talked about old times and good memories.

Then everyone said goodnight, and Jack and Lisa were left alone in that house, staring at each other. Two lonely people terribly aware of the wall between them; two people exhausted from the strain of pretending to be happily married.

The cracks that had always existed in their relationship now had become deep crevasses. Jack was frequently gone on business trips. For years their conflicts had been resolved only by his lengthy absences.

Lisa had tried to build a life of her own, getting a job and widening her circle of friends. But that wasn't enough anymore. She needed more, and she had begun to wonder if she could ever get it from her husband.

Jack tried; he sincerely wanted the marriage to work. But he wasn't very good at communicating his feelings. He tended to look for an intellectual answer to everything, reading books and pondering abstract questions, while Lisa wanted emotional support.

And Lisa, an incurable romantic, had allowed her affections to wander. She'd been crazy about Jack and almost worshiped him. But what before she had regarded as great wisdom, she now viewed as a way of Jack's controlling her.

Jack tried to be more supportive. But by now Lisa had grown quite cold. Why should he keep trying, he told himself, if his wife wasn't going to respond? And Lisa kept questioning Jack's sincerity; he was just trying to control her.

Neither of them wanted a divorce. Their religious and personal convictions had never allowed that option. And yet they couldn't find the will to stay together. They kept groping around in the dark, bumping into each other, less and less able to trust, seeing more and more fatal flaws in the other—and little hope for change.

Jack and Lisa's story hits close to home for a lot of people today. More and more marriages are falling apart after years of attempting to stay together. Marriages are breaking in the middle. Couples are giving up on ten, fifteen, or twenty years of a relationship.

Many counselors believe marriages become especially vulnerable after the kids grow up. Some partners find that raising their children was about the only thing they had in common.

Other observers talk about the strains that the mid-life crisis brings on. A lot of people who've achieved success in their jobs wake up one morning, look around, and ask, "Is this all there is?"

There's another factor that contributes to marriages breaking apart in the middle. Let's be honest. In some homes, it's the women who've made the sacrifices, have put up with their husbands' problems, and have done what it takes to keep the family together. These women, today, are tired of playing that role; too often their long-suffering love turns them into victims of abuse. A lot of them are just plain tired out and upset, and they're not going to take it anymore.

All these forces pressing in on couples in mid-life create one great cry from the heart: "Something has got to change!" I'm sure you've heard a friend or acquaintance say, "I just can't go on living this way; I'm going to snap." Perhaps it's your own secret cry: "I can't take it anymore; something has got to change!"

For couples under pressure, the obvious answer seems to be: "Change your marriage partner. He or she is the one causing all the problems. What you've got to do is change the person staring back at you across the breakfast table."

Let's face it. Sometimes victims *do* need to be rescued. Sometimes abusers need to be directly and openly confronted. Anyone with a pattern of verbal or physical abuse who refuses to seek help is destroying his or her marriage.

Unfortunately, the language of abuse is now applied to all kinds of situations. Criticizing or nagging is sometimes viewed as verbal assault. Some begin to see manipulation or an attempt to control lurking behind every request or comment. People can find passive-aggressive behavior in every silence, every gesture. Common faults can be blown up into great crimes with the language of abuse.

There definitely *are* people who compulsively try to control their spouses, always putting them down, always trying to restrict their friends and interests. But the vast majority of troubled couples are simply caught in a web of trying to control each other in big and little ways. The road to marital pain and suffering is a two-way street. That's why I'd like to suggest an alternative to simply changing a spouse. It's true, something has got to change! But it's not the marriage that's somehow to blame. It's the people in it. People need to change themselves, not just their partners.

Hoping that the next person down the line will make you happy is to hope against hope. You'll still be carrying the same baggage into the next relationship. You'll still have your same habits, your same compulsions, your same tendencies. You'll still have the same unresolved hurts.

It's people that need to change.

Listen to what counselors say who've talked to hundreds of people on their second go-around. They say that the most typical comment is: "If I'd known then what I know now, I would have worked harder—much harder—to keep my first marriage going."

When our marriage is under pressure, we're apt to see everything that's wrong, everything that's a problem—except our own behavior.

A New York therapist who'd worked with fractured relationships decided to use a novel technique. He began videotaping the sessions each couple had with him and then giving the couple an instant replay. The results were remarkable. Husbands and wives saw themselves on the screen exactly as they were—body language, intonation, gestures, and all. The tapes were so revealing that many couples began to resolve their disputes almost immediately. For the first time in their lives they got an answer to the question few of us ask: "What's it like being married to me?"

What *is* it like? People need to change themselves, not just their marriage partners. Any relationship can be salvaged if husband and wife are willing, first, to let God help them change.

Now admittedly, it's one thing to talk about change, and quite another thing to actually do it. After you've spent years in unhealthy ruts, it may seem impossible to get out of them. And you may well believe that the person across the breakfast table won't ever really change. But listen again to this familiar promise from the Old Testament and try to apply it to your own marriage. Ezekiel gives hope for troubled, hardened hearts in any marriage relationship. Through the prophet, God says, " 'I will give you a new heart and put a new spirit within you; I will take the heart of stone out of your flesh and give you a heart of flesh' " (Ezekiel 36:26, NKJV).

A heart of flesh. Yes, damaged marriages can make us hard-hearted; they can set our worst qualities in stone. But that's what God's grace is for; that's what the promise of a new heart is for.

The New Testament fairly bursts with the theme of radical change. And friends, it doesn't apply just to drunkards in the gutter or to profane atheists. It applies to our marriages as well.

Read Paul's prayer in Colossians: "That you may have a walk worthy of the Lord, fully pleasing Him, being fruitful in every good work and increasing in the knowledge of God; strengthened with all might, according to His glorious power, for all patience and longsuffering with joy" (Colossians 1:10, 11).

"Strengthened with all might, according to his glorious power." God gives us the power to change; the power to move out of our ruts. Let me give you a few encouraging examples of how this happens. Here are positive ways that couples can deal with what appear to be incompatible traits.

Bill is a quiet, reserved emergency-room physician who likes to ski and scuba-dive. Linda is a counselor who's very open and demonstrative about her feelings. Bill likes to take physical risks in the great out-of-doors. Linda took emotional risks, always saying just what she felt, hoping Bill would understand.

This couple was going in opposite directions—fast. The more Linda expressed her feelings, the more Bill withdrew. The more Bill withdrew, the more Linda wanted to slam pots and pans.

Finally the two went to counseling and discovered a wonderful concept—the way to help their relationship was to help each other. They could learn and grow from their differences. Bill came to see that it was OK to express emotions with those you trust. He opened up more. And Linda learned to think before she spoke. Eventually she learned to enjoy some of Bill's favorite outdoor activities.

A reserved person and an expressive person can either push each other further and further apart or they can learn from each other.

Marjorie and Steve experienced constant friction in their marriage because of incompatible traits. She was very outgoing. He was painfully shy. Usually that meant that Marjorie would beg Steve to attend some party, he'd make up some excuse, and she'd have to go by herself—alone and furious.

But instead of just changing partners they tried changing themselves. Steve started attending a few parties. Slowly he grew more sociable. Marjorie learned there were some activities she could enjoy quietly at home. Instead of becoming more and more extreme in their traits, these two people became more whole and healthy as human beings. They learned from each other.

Here's wonderful advice from the apostle James on how couples can become more teachable: "Let every man be swift to hear, slow to speak, slow to wrath" (James 1:19, NKJV).

That's it in a nutshell. Quick to listen, slow to speak, slow to become angry. That makes us teachable. Instead of just changing our spouses, we need to see if we can learn from our partner. What we see as an incompatible trait in the other person may be trying to tell us something important about ourselves.

Sometimes, of course, it's not just a question of different traits or different interests. Sometimes marriages deteriorate because of real problem behaviors. Take Lionel, for example. He was something of a malcontent who found fault with everyone and everything. His wife, Jean, was the usual target of his complaints. For fifteen years she tried her very best to cater to Lionel's every whim. She tried so hard to make him happy.

Well, Jean finally burned out and went for counseling. But as she did so, she learned something very important. She learned that no one can *make* another person happy. She was not responsible for her husband's happiness; he was.

When Jean accepted this fact, she became more relaxed and outgoing. The pressure was off. And Lionel woke up himself when he realized Jean no longer accepted the blame for everything. He began to occupy his time more productively.

Sometimes we need to detach ourselves from the problem behavior of the other person. We can become enablers, helping a spouse to continue in his or her bad habits. When Jean decided to stop doing that, she found leverage—a positive force to lift her husband. She found that behaving in a healthy way herself nudged her husband toward healthier behavior.

For some time, Donna and Ray had been caught in a pattern known as the "nag-and-withdraw" syndrome. Donna would nag Ray about not putting his things away and not helping her around the house enough. Ray would become silent and withdrawn. That would drive his wife up the wall, and she'd nag more.

After they went for help, Ray recognized that what Donna wanted more than anything else was physical attention from him. Her nagging was really an effort to spark some show of emotion. Ray realized that he had leverage. By showing a little more spontaneous affection he could short-circuit the nagging problem. Ray and Donna began meeting each other's needs instead of driving each other up the wall.

The writer of Hebrews gives some advice which is especially fitting for couples wrestling with problem behavior. "Exhort one another daily . . . lest any of you be hardened through the deceitfulness of sin" (Hebrews 3:13, NKJV). This verse pictures the two directions a relationship can go. Spouses can either encourage each other or harden each other. Those problem behaviors, those deceitful sins, will harden and alienate marriage partners unless they find some leverage, unless they find a positive way to encourage. And often that is accomplished by a person displaying healthy behavior himself.

Later in the book of Hebrews the writer urges: "And let us consider one another in order to stir up love and good works" (Hebrews 10:24, NKJV). If you're just reacting to your spouse's problem behavior, the marriage will harden.

But if you concentrate on your own positive behavior, chances are your spouses will be moved "toward love and good deeds."

Recently, *Psychology Today* reported on a study of 300 couples who had stayed together for many years. They were asked to talk about why they had enduring and happy marriages. Can you guess the most frequently-named reason? It was simply this: these individuals *liked* their spouses as persons; they viewed their partners as their best friends.

Now this basic attitude may seem impossible to couples whose relationship has deteriorated over the years. They think they've seen too much; they remember all the ways their spouse has hurt them. But stop for a moment. All of us at one point liked our spouse as a person. When we chose to marry him or her, we saw things that attracted us; we saw things to love. Our bride or groom had weaknesses and faults, but we didn't look at those. In the enthusiasm of our first love, we noticed only the good things.

We may not be able to capture that initial infatuation, but we *can* recapture that initial perspective. We can make a conscious choice to look at our partner's good qualities. Remember, no matter what our circumstances, we always have a choice.

We can focus either on the things we don't like or on the things we do like. What we look at can make an enormous difference.

A little gratitude goes a long, long way, believe me. Focusing on positive qualities makes them expand. So please, don't just change your partner if your present mate seems unsatisfactory. Most people simply end up with someone with a slightly different mix of bad and good qualities. Instead, change your perspective. Change what you focus on. This is most effective, of course, if both partners promise to do that together. Two people looking for the best in each other can overcome almost any obstacle.

Today we're experiencing an epidemic of the wrong kind of change—people changing their partners when what really needs to change is the human heart. So please remember to ask that all-important question: "What's it like—being married to me?"

Please remember that God can take out our hearts of stone and replace them with hearts of flesh. With God's resources at your disposal, no situation is hopeless. So start learning from your partner's differences, instead of just criticizing them. Start using the right kind of leverage to change problem behaviors. And start focusing on the positive qualities in your mate that once held your devoted attention.

Please don't just look for a magic solution to your problems in a new face. There are people who go through their whole lives, moving from one relationship to another, thinking happiness is just around the corner, and never, never dealing with the real problems in their own hearts, never facing what really needs to change. Don't fall into that trap.

By God's grace we can all change. We can change ourselves instead of just trying to change our partners. Let's make that commitment now as we pray:

Father in heaven, we need help. Marriages are deteriorating; relationships are falling apart. And sometimes the walls built up between us seem insurmountable. Sometimes it seems there's just too much hurt and anger to overcome. But we acknowledge right now that You can give us the support and the power to make positive changes in our lives. So we ask for the strength that the Holy Spirit alone can give. We ask for Your divine energy. Please help us move our marriages out of their ruts and into Your hands. In Jesus' name, Amen.

What Trevor Left Behind

Trevor was "everybody's child." From the time he was an infant, people seemed to notice something uniquely endearing about him. Baby sitters always wanted to keep him. Somehow, Trevor made himself everyone's friend. He was more thoughtful and thankful than most kids—the only child I've ever heard of whose Christmas wish list started with: "Things to give."

And most remarkably, Trevor possessed a natural, spontaneous, unreserved love for God.

So how do you explain an inoperable brain tumor? And how do you explain this precious life wasting away? How could God take such a child—or any child? And how can those who are left behind possibly cope?

In this chapter, you'll hear an unforgettable story—straight from a mother's heart.

They had done everything they could—the doctors, the nurses, the specialists—but Trevor Richert was quickly slipping away. They could tell by his complexion, by his shallow breathing that the long struggle was almost over. One of the nurses there turned to Trevor's mom, Sandy, keeping her vigil, and asked, "Would you like to hold him?"

They all knew it would be for the last time.

So Sandy sat in a large chair, and two nurses gently

lifted the boy from his bed and carried him over to his mom's lap.

Sandy would never forget those final moments, feeling the warmth of her child—the little warmth that remained—remembering their precious times together. It seemed now like such a little time. She remembered the many, many people who had prayed so earnestly—apparently in vain—for her boy's healing and wondered how on earth could she possibly live without this child. How could life go on without Trevor?

Would you have an answer to that question—watching this mother hold her son for the last time? Do we have any answers at all for such a tragedy?

What are people supposed to do when they've invested all their hopes and dreams and prayers and all their energy and all their love in this one human being who needs them—and that human being is taken away?

What do we do when we pray earnestly, persistently, desperately—and God seems to say only, "No"? Not only that, but He seems to rip out our hearts.

Well, many people have tried very hard to come up with answers that make some sense out of tragedy, to come up with answers to comfort the grieving. And often those answers seem pretty trite to those on the inside of the tragedy.

In this chapter, I'd like you to meet someone who's been there, someone who's struggled with all the emotions. And I simply want her to tell her story. I'd like to introduce Sandy Wyman-Richert, Trevor's mom.

Mark: From time to time, I've heard you share Trevor's story, and every time, Sandy, it's touched my own heart. You have some unique insights into sorrow and suffering. Share with us a little bit about when you first began to notice that something was wrong with Trevor.

Sandy: About four years ago, he began to show some very subtle symptoms—dizziness, getting carsick easily, having some double vision off and on. These things would come and go, and the doctors weren't concerned about them at that time. But they began to be more progressive. So we began to make the rounds of specialists. Originally, they felt that he had encephalitis, just an inflammation of the brain, and that he would recover from that.

After he was in the hospital for a couple of weeks of treatment for that condition, the doctors sent him home. He was home for about three weeks in a hospital bed; we were trying to rehabilitate him. By this time, he had to lie on his right side continuously. For a couple of months, he'd been lying only on his right side because he had violent dizziness and difficulty speaking and difficulty swallowing.

But he never complained. He always had a smile on his face, and he'd work his food down the side of his mouth. Then one morning, he couldn't swallow his pills or get his food down; he's the one who looked at me and said, "Mommy, I don't think I'm getting any better. I think you need to call the doctor."

So we readmitted him to the hospital. It was when the fifth MRI scan was done that the doctors were able to finally see the brain stem widening. With this particular type of tumor, it mixes like putting creamer in a hot drink, and you can't isolate it. So the doctors came in and shared the news with us that we probably just had a few weeks.

Mark: What kind of emotions did you go through at that time?

Sandy: At that moment, I felt like I'd been run over by a truck. I'm a nurse, and I've worked many years in intensive care units around people who are nearing the end of their life for one reason or another. So I knew, clinically, what was coming. But as a mother, I was helpless to stop it.

My life flashed before me. I'm a minister's daughter, so I summoned up all of my life history—of who I had believed God to be—and started recounting all of my sins and confessing them and doing all these things that you think puts you in that magical place where you're going to make God come through and do what you want Him to do for you.

Mark: Did you believe that God was going to heal Trevor?

Sandy: That's a good question. You know, I hoped with every ounce in me that God would do such a thing. And I still believe that He does heal today. But I was raised to believe, and I still believe, that He would do what is in our best interest to do. That is, He has a purpose and a plan for our lives and the methods that He uses to accomplish that plan are a mystery to us. So I believed that that is what would happen.

However, my prayer then, had to be, "Please help me to accept whatever the outcome will be." That would be my struggle—to accept His methods.

Mark: Were other people praying for Trevor? Did you organize some prayer groups?

Sandy: Thousands of people were praying. Hundreds of churches across the country were praying for Trevor. His little first-grade classroom prayed every day. We had two all-night prayer vigils at our church in Arroyo Grande, California, where people came all night, ate a few snacks, but claimed Scripture and sang songs and prayed all night.

But I think that if it was God's intention to heal Trevor physically, He would have done it from Trevor's prayers alone. If you could have heard them—they were so sweet! He'd say, "Dear Jesus, I don't want to die, but I want to trust You. Please come and place Your hand on the part of my head that isn't well and make me well so I can go home.

And help me not to be afraid." But he always said, "I want to trust You." His prayers were so sweet.

Mark: Sandy, as these prayer vigils went on, did you notice any change in Trevor's condition?

Sandy: Well, the interesting thing is that the harder we prayed and the more people that prayed, the worse he got. I remember cornering my dad one day in the hall of the hospital; I was crying out loud, and I said, "Dad, this is ridiculous! The harder we pray, the quicker he's going."

In retrospect, of course, there are many answers to prayer, as you look back—answers that are not the precise thing you prayed for, but that were answers all along, nonetheless.

So Trevor began to get worse and, in fact, one week into that hospitalization, he developed a kidney stone, which is very rare in children. And he began having very acute pain. He never complained, he'd just draw up his legs and point to his tummy.

I was very angry with God about the kidney stone. I couldn't understand why he had to have that pain on top of everything else he'd been through. As the next week went by and this pain got worse, we eventually had to come to a decision to medicate him to a level of comfort that would relieve that pain. And that level of comfort—the medication it took to do that—allowed him to quietly go to sleep. He had said to me a few days before, "Mommy, if I die I don't want it be in a bad way."

And I said, "Trevie, what does that mean?"

He said, "Well, I don't want to be choking, and I don't want to be in bad pain."

I said, "Honey, if this is going to be your journey, then let's pray together that God will make it something that will be peaceful for you."

So that's what we did. And here, the kidney stone, that I was so angry about, became the greatest blessing. Because we were allowed to simply medicate him, and he went to sleep.

Mark: In those last days before his death, you spent a lot of personal time with Trevor. What kind of intimate, mother-son time did you have?

Sandy: Oh, I tell you, those are memories for a lifetime. Perhaps I did more loving in those two weeks than I might have done in a lifetime. We did a lot of crafts together, and we sang a lot of songs. Trevor really loved music. The first week, we started out with "Take Me Out to the Ball Game" and "Rubber Ducky" and things like that. But eventually, he began asking for prayer three times a day. And I know now that he knew he was getting worse.

Then he wanted to sing, "Do Lord" and "My Home's in Heaven." His favorite was "He's Able." So we did a lot of singing. We prayed together a lot. People would come to visit, and Trevor always wanted to make sure that I made out a list of people to write Thank-you notes to. That was very important to him.

But we spent a lot of family time. And I spent time memorizing every freckle and eyelash; I just couldn't imagine, of course, what life would be without him.

Mark: You told me a story about a butterfly. What was that about?

Sandy: When Trevor was home those three weeks between hospitalizations, he had sent away on his birthday for a "butterfly garden." Now, I'd never done this before. These little larvae came in the mail—five live larvae in a jar that eat this brown gooey stuff on the bottom of the container. They go up to the top, spin their cocoons on the filter paper, and eventually emerge as butterflies.

Well, when Trevor was hospitalized the last time, he was very concerned that he would not live long enough to see his butterflies come out. So I went home one day (it was an hour-and-a-half drive to our house from the hospital) and brought back these butterfly larvae knocking around in the back of the van! I didn't really think they'd make it, but I brought them to the hospital.

And the news went out all over the wards that there was a little boy on pediatrics that was growing butterflies. People would come in every day asking, "Are they out yet? Are they out yet?" And he just loved that.

One day, they all emerged, one after the other, little painted lady butterflies. And we watched them in the viewing box for a couple days. Then we went up to the sixth floor of the hospital, which was the roof with a gorgeous view, and we let them go. One by one they flew away.

Trevor looked at me, and he said without any prompting, "Mommy, the larvae, the caterpillars, are like our life here on earth. And the cocoons are like when we die, and we sleep. And the butterflies are like when Jesus comes, and we go to heaven."

Mark: What insights for a seven-year-old boy!

Sandy: What a sermon!

Mark: God placed in his heart, no doubt, a sense of the fact that there was something beyond this life. What kind of influence did Trevor have on nurses, on physicians, on other people in the hospital?

Sandy: You know, that is remarkable. Even on the people who were praying for him, yet didn't know him, the influence was so amazing. Once again I set God's agenda for Him. I thought, "What a marvelous opportunity, God!" I said to Him, "This is a condition that no doctor can heal. Thousands are praying. A whole community knows about it. And so here, God, is such an opportunity for you to do this miracle that Trevor can talk about for the rest of his life!"

How often we take a blank piece of paper, and we write out God's agenda on it. Then we sign it, and we graciously give it to Him. But what we need to do is to take a blank piece of paper and sign it at the bottom and give it to Him. And until I did that, I had no peace.

Probably nine or ten of the nurses who cared for Trevor during that month at the hospital drove an hour and a half to his memorial service and were touched deeply by our family's experience there at the hospital.

Mark: How did the end of his life on this earth come?

Sandy: On a Friday night he had a small seizure. Some of us had gone out to dinner, and when we came back, all the nurses and doctors were around his bed. My heart skipped eighty-two beats! But he slept till the next morning.

When we talked with him in the morning, it was as if he had had a small stroke. He began trying to talk to us, and sounds came out, but he couldn't form any words. He began to cry, and I began to cry. His brain was just as smart; it was just that his motor skills were not functioning as they should.

So I gave him a clipboard to write on, but the letters he made were all on top of each other. He looked at me, and I looked at him. Then he looked at the eight-by-ten family portrait that we had in his room, and he motioned for it. He touched everybody's face on the picture, and he began to cry.

I said, "Trevie, do you want to see the other children today?" And he nodded, "Yes."

The next day was Father's Day, and they were going to come anyway. So we brought them down early. We began to summon the family. Everyone arrived and was able to hug Trevor and be with him. Then the pain from the kidney stone kicked up very badly. So we had to make a decision to relieve his pain.

I told him, "Trevie, this pain is really bad, and you have been so very brave. We're able to give you some medication that will take care of the pain and make you comfortable."

He looked at me, and his eyes got sort of big. I knew that he knew what I was saying. And I said, "Is that OK with you?"

And he squeezed my hand and kind of gave me a thumbs-up sign. And so that's what happened. We began to medicate him. We spent two days playing praise music in the background and taking turns lying down with him and loving on him and talking to him.

Then I had that chance to hold him. I have never in my entire life felt God's presence literally as close to me as in those moments when I was holding Trevor. I knew He understood how I felt.

Mark: How did you work through the anger, the bitterness? Or was there any? Was it all just, "Praise the Lord! I'm all right with whatever you want to happen, God"? Did you have that kind of resolute faith or did you experience anger with God at some point?

Sandy: Well, I was raised to practice that resolute faith, but I'd never been brought to a place where I had to apply it. This was very different. And so everything kind of goes back to square one. Either what you've talked about and believed is absolutely true or it's absolutely not.

You have a choice—whether to act as if it is true and act on it or not. You know, you can choose to become angry, bitter, or resentful, or you can choose to believe that God is still who He says He is and that He's operating out of love.

So I made that conscious choice even though I didn't fully understand what was happening. I found the text that says God gives us a peace that passes understanding, and now I understand what that means. It means that God gives me a peace that takes me beyond the need to understand.

I think the best advice I could probably give to anyone who is going through this is to lean into it. Don't run from it; don't try to escape it. It'll take you to places you've never been before. There's nothing you can do to bring back what you've lost. Make a choice to continue to trust anyway, and God will give you what you need to keep going.

Mark: Trevor was not healed, but it seems to me that people around him were healed; their hearts were healed. It seems to me that God did something in your own life. What did God do through you, and for you, in this experience?

Sandy: I think that we are very obsessed, as human beings, with alleviating or avoiding pain in our life. I think we're more focused on the satisfaction God can give than we are focused on God Himself. So I've learned to pursue Him. When I got very real with Him about my feelings, then He got very real with me. I read something that says that when He seems the most silent, He's actually being the most intimate.

So, I can't tell you enough about how very real this experience has been for me. I think it's a great miracle when God heals physically. But if you think about it, all those Christ healed, when He was here on earth, eventually died. He came to reveal something about the heart of the Father and His own heart, and I believe He still performs physical miracles today and we ought to storm the gates of heaven in prayer about that.

But the fact is that oftentimes He does not heal physically. What He desires most is the healing of our hearts. And if you will allow it, He gives you the strength to determine to keep trusting. Then He gives you the compassion to turn around and help somebody else who is hurting, too.

Mark: Sandy, your testimony rings true-to-life. As you look at the New Testament, God didn't heal everybody.

There were scores of people that weren't healed. Has He built your faith, your trust, your confidence in Him through this experience?

Sandy: Absolutely! Because the experience of the gospel is not one that you can just talk about in theory. It's not about theory; it's about experience.

As I have been willing to share this story with others, they have often shared their stories in return. And we have found a common bond in woundedness, but we have also found a common bond in hope because we have a blessed reunion to look forward to someday.

Mark: Thank you so much, Sandy. Your story inspires us because it helps us look beyond this life with its sorrows, its disappointments, and its heartaches, to the healing that will come when Jesus Christ returns. Then there will be no sickness or suffering, no babies laid in tombs again, and we look forward to that day. That's the real hope, when Jesus comes.

There's a God who, in the deepest pain of our lives, understands—a God who's there in the context of our sorrow. His Son went through immense sorrow. God was there, and He's there in your sorrow, friend.

Whatever your sorrow, whatever your anguish, whatever the trouble that's throwing a shadow over your life—bring it to Jesus, right now. Don't just keep it shut up inside. Don't let it harden into bitterness. Please bring it to the One who gave us all things in the gift of His Son and let the healing begin.

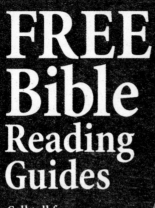
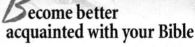